THE HOW AND WHY WONDER® BOOK OF

The CIVIL WAR

Written by EARL SCHENCK MIERS
Illustrated by LEONARD VOSBURGH
Editorial Production: DONALD D. WOLF

Edited under the supervision of
Dr. Paul E. Blackwood,
Washington, D. C.

Text and illustrations approved by
Oakes A. White, Brooklyn Children's Museum, Brooklyn, New York

PRICE/STERN/SLOAN
Publishers, Inc., Los Angeles
1987

Introduction

With the publication of this book on the Civil War, *The How and Why Wonder® Books* extends a growing list of titles to the field of history. Children, parents and teachers who have learned to know these publications through the science titles will be pleased to know that books on other subjects are now included.

In an exciting way this book tells the *how* of the war as soldiers and generals engage in battle after battle in the North and in the South of our struggling, young Nation. In a warmly sympathetic mood, it also tells the *why* of the war, showing the way differences in beliefs, values and economic necessities led to conflict.

The personal and military strengths and weaknesses of Union and Confederate leaders are forthrightly portrayed as they have a bearing on the outcome of the war. You feel again the greatness of Lee and Lincoln. You sense the determination of McClellan, Grant, Stonewall Jackson and others. You feel human power at work as the war ebbs and flows and finally ends.

Paul E. Blackwood

Dr. Blackwood is a professional employee in the U. S. Office of Education. This book was edited by him in his private capacity and no official support or endorsement by the Office of Education is intended or should be inferred.

Copyright © 1961 by Price/Stern/Sloan Publishers, Inc.
Published by Price/Stern/Sloan Publishers, Inc.
360 North La Cienega Blvd., Los Angeles, CA 90048

ISBN 0-8431-4251-0

Library of Congress Catalogue Card Number: 61-1742

How and Why Wonder® Books is a trademark of Price/Stern/Sloan Publishers, Inc.

Contents

Southern cotton plantations, cultivated largely by slaves, produced abundant crops of cotton for northern mills.

Our Country a Hundred Years Ago

Why was it like a young giant, waking up?

Our country, one hundred years ago, was like a growing boy or girl whose arms, legs, head and body sometimes acted as though they were strangers. As a nation, we were still painfully, awkwardly young. Only seventy-one years before, George Washington had been elected first President of thirteen states that, with tongues in their cheeks, had agreed to try living together under a government elected by the people.

Yet we had done better than anybody had expected. We were now a nation of thirty-four states and our flag proudly spanked in the breeze upon the shores of the blue Pacific. Along the rivers and through the mountain passes that hardy frontiersmen had followed to discover a vast continent, we had begun to build railroads and highways. Across still unsettled territories where wild animals and hostile Indians roamed, Pony Express riders carried the mail between East and West. Proud steamboats churned the Mississippi, and adventuresome homesteaders broke the hard sod of Kansas with their crude wooden plows, and along the Texas border a colonel named Robert E. Lee chased Indians, and across the undeveloped West men strung the wires of the newfangled telegraph.

So, as one country, we were beginning to come together, but we were only beginning. America a hundred years ago remained pretty much what you saw with your own eyes and heard with your own ears.

4

Cheap water power aided New England factories.

For example, since in New England there were many falls in the rivers that could supply cheap power, it was logical to build factories and the New England boy and girl grew up in an America where people held jobs making products and shipping them to the markets of the world.

For another example, since the land in the South was suitable for growing cotton, plantations cultivated by slaves had developed as a natural way of life, and Southern boys and girls were taught to accept slaves with kindness and understanding as their rightful property.

A third class of Americans, restless and ambitious, moved into the undeveloped territories seeking a new start in life. If they came from the South they brought Southern ideas, and if they came from New England they brought New England ideas. Both believed that

The steamboats plied along America's waterways.

5

they were normal, decent fellows at heart, and since they had the gumption to push out on their own they didn't much like to be shoved around by anyone.

It was a wonderful country, really — full of life and rich with promise. Already it had developed great cities — New York, Philadelphia, Baltimore, Boston, Cincinnati, Louisville and that booming young upstart on the shores of Lake Michigan, Chicago. From all the countries of Europe people came to America, seeking freedom and a new life. St. Louis, a city of red brick houses on the banks of the Mississippi, was a good example of what such migrations could mean. From fifty to sixty thousand Germans now lived in St. Louis— loyal Americans to the core who in another year would march off to war.

It was a go-ahead, pick-yourself-up-by-the-bootstraps country. Gold in the Rockies, gold in the Sierra Nevada — nobody knew how rich the land might

be. It was a country that could grow corn and wheat and graze great herds of cattle, a country of unbelievable beauty to make a lump come into your throat, a country where people worked hard and played hard and on Sunday put on their best clothes and went to church morning, noon and night. Its

Homestead laws made possible the settlement of public lands in Kansas and other territories.

giant, waking up, and now and then finding a hen that could lay a golden egg. People awoke in the morning to a sense of adventure just around the corner — an Indian raid maybe, or a new gold strike, or the never failing excitement of a steamboat coming round the bend.

And yet it was a troubled country. Growth brought problems — people who began wondering if what they heard in church on Sunday they practiced on Monday, and if the old ways were necessarily the best ways, and if with all the angry talking that was going on there wouldn't be some angry fighting sooner or later.

In time of course there was a lot of fighting, and this is the story of how it came about — and why — and how it all turned out — and again why.

folk heroes were Johnny Appleseed planting his orchards in the wilderness and Paul Bunyan creating another lake wherever he stepped and Mike Fink spinning his yarns and fighting with the other keel boatmen on the Ohio.

The country one hundred years ago was still largely unsettled. It was a

Colonel Robert E. Lee fought off Indians along the Texas border in days before the Civil War.

7

The Gathering Storm

A Connecticut Yankee was really at the bottom of all the trouble that developed, although this fact wasn't his fault. When, seventy-one years before, Washington had become our first President, we had believed that slavery would soon die out. For a number of years societies working to free the slaves were far more numerous in the South than in the North. But then along came that Connecticut Yankee — Eli Whitney — who invented a machine for separating cotton from its seed. With Whitney's "cotton gin" a crop could be harvested more quickly and with much higher profits, and when in England at about this time machinery was invented for spinning fine cotton thread, the South could sell all the cotton it could grow.

The South soon forgot it ever had wanted to free its slaves. Indeed, argued those who needed slaves to grow more and more cotton, look at how well we use the Negro. When he is sick or too old to work, we care for him. Now, in contrast, take your white "wage slave" in New England and let him grow ill or old and what happens? You kick him out to starve!

But the torment of mind and heart that once had haunted even the South lived on. Slavery was not right. No man should be another man's master or live by the sweat of another man's brow. In the North and in a large part of the booming Midwest, where slaves were not needed (nor wanted), the movement to end slavery grew enormously.

For a long time the statesmen of the nation tried to keep this great conflict of mind and heart within check. Whenever a "slave" state was admitted to the Union, a "free" state also was admitted. Boundaries were set beyond which, we said, slavery could not pass.

The nation kept growing, however. Like steam in a boiler, the pressure mounted to sweep aside such restrictions and tempers broke under the heat of this pressure. Northerners who opposed slavery were called troublemakers, stealers of slaves, tyrants who wanted to rule the country. In Kansas open warfare broke out between those who supported and those who opposed slavery as the territory organized for admission to the Union. And in Illinois a strong voice spoke up, warning the nation: "We cannot be half slave and half free." The voice belonged to Abraham Lincoln.

In the election of 1860 the people came face to face with a decision. Two Democrats ran for President—Stephen A. Douglas of Illinois, who said that it was up to the settlers of a territory to decide whether they wished to be a slave state or a free state, and John C. Breckinridge of Kentucky, who believed that no territory had a right to forbid slavery. As the Republican candidate, Lincoln said he would not interfere with slavery where it then existed but it should extend no further. The Union Party candidate, John Bell of Tennessee, ignored the issue of slavery.

The two Democratic candidates drew a total popular vote of 2,226,738 against 1,866,452 for Lincoln, but Lincoln amassed 180 electoral votes against their 84 — a smashing victory. Quickly the supporters of slavery reacted. No "Black Republican" was going to tell the South how it must live!

Abe Lincoln was elected the 16th President in 1860.

Military companies began to form, taking such names as the "Cherokee Lincoln Killers" to make absolutely clear where they stood. Nobody really wanted war. But war was what the nation faced.

Southern boys organized into military units.

What was the
principle Lincoln
wouldn't give up?

Six Critical Weeks

The South moved swiftly to break with the Union and establish its own government. Amid the tolling of church bells and the joyous shouts of people, South Carolina seceded on December 22, 1860, and by early February six other states had followed its example — Georgia, Mississippi, Alabama, Florida, Louisiana, and Texas. In Montgomery, Alabama, delegates from these states met that month to form the Confederate States of America and to write a constitution that recognized slaves as property. For President they selected Jefferson Davis, a stanch states-righter from Mississippi, and except for Fort Sumter in Charleston Harbor, Fort Pickens in Pensacola Bay and two small forts off the Florida coast all Federal forts, arsenals, customhouses and lighthouses were seized in the seceding states.

Montgomery, the capital of the new nation, went wild with excitement. Think of it! Without shedding a drop of blood — and even before Old Abe Lincoln had reached Washington — Southern independence had been achieved! But one thorn still stung Southern pride. On Christmas night in Charleston Harbor a small Federal force under Major Robert Anderson had moved unexpectedly from antiquated Fort Moultrie (which was impossible to defend) to Fort Sumter (which only could be approached by water and which controlled the sea lanes into the harbor). An insult, raged the South. A symbol of national honor, replied the North.

Lincoln, traveling from his home in Springfield, Illinois to become President of a now divided nation, tried to appear undisturbed by the impending crisis. From one whistle stop to the next, he struck the same theme: "We are not enemies, but friends." Given time to think through the problem, he believed Americans would respond to "the better angels" of their spirits. Born in Kentucky, grown to manhood in Indiana, matured on the prairies of Illinois, he had a sublime faith in the strength of the nation — and in the hard, good sense of the common people. Yet, now and then, there came a flash of a streak in Lincoln that revealed he would not back down on one principle. In Indianapolis he asked: "What is the peculiar sacredness of a state?" At any cost the Union must be held together!

On March 4, 1861 tenseness lay over crowded Washington, D. C. At noon the retiring President, James Buchanan, called at Willard's Hotel to escort Lincoln to the ceremonies that would make him the sixteenth President. Old Winfield Scott, the General of the Army, was worried sick over the many threats that had been made against Lincoln's life — threats like the one from a correspondent called "Vindex" who informed Lincoln that "a sworn Band of 10" had resolved "to shoot you from the south side of the Avenue in the inaugural procession."

General Scott took no chances. Soldiers stood on rooftops and at street crossings to guard against possible assassins. Expert marksmen were stationed at each window where the wings of the Capitol flanked the inaugural stand. Lincoln, wearing a new black suit, arose erect and unruffled, and spoke from his heart. "One section of our country believes slavery is *right,* and ought to be extended," he said, "while the other believes it is *wrong,* and ought not to be extended. This is the only substantial dispute." Chief Justice Taney, looking like "a galvanized corpse," administered the oath.

But trouble a-plenty awaited Lincoln. Provisions were running low at Fort Sumter and its small Federal garrison would soon be starved out unless supplies were delivered. Six critical weeks followed with each day filled with mounting war talk. The Secretary of State, William H. Seward, speaking off the record, assured Confederate commissioners in Washington that Sumter would be abandoned. Meanwhile Colonel Robert E. Lee was offered field command of the Northern forces should war come, but he declined. Lee would fight only in defense of his beloved Virginia, yet he did not deny that he hated slavery.

"If I owned four million slaves," Lee told a friend, "I would cheerfully sacrifice them for the preservation of the Union."

Seward's promise that Sumter would be abandoned was not fulfilled, and Southern patience neared the breaking-point. Both Virginia and Missouri voted against immediate secession, proof that if Lincoln was allowed enough time to stall on the Sumter crisis the Confederacy might collapse under its own weight. In Charleston the "hot-heads" screamed

for action. But Lincoln could delay no longer. He must attempt to provision Sumter, and so the South learned that Federal ships were at sea for that very purpose. Orders were sent to General Pierre Gustave Toutant Beauregard, commanding the Confederate forces in Charleston. Demand at once the surrender of the fort, those orders instructed. And if the demand were refused? In that event, the orders continued, "proceed in such a manner as you may determine, to reduce it."

Lincoln took the oath of office despite death threats.

Why couldn't the warships save Fort Sumter?

War Over A Fort

The demand was refused. And so, at 4:30 on the morning of April 12, 1861, a single mortar boomed out in Charleston Harbor. Many eyes followed the burning fuse of the shell as it arched among the twinkling stars. For a moment it seemed to hang suspended in the night sky, then faster and faster the shell descended. It struck with a flash inside the fort, bursting into a hundred fragments.

To save ammunition, the Federal forces waited until daylight to return the fire, and then only an occasional shell was thrown into the city. Through the day, as the uneven duel went on, jubilant Charlestonians crowded rooftops and cheered their cannoneers with each new burst of flame within the fort.

A Federal gunner in Sumter, beholding this throng, growled to a mate: "If it's war they like, then 'tis war they shall get!" He aimed a forty-two pounder at the spectators and let fly. The shot bounded fifty yards above the heads of the onlookers and they were soon scampering for cover.

But this was a small triumph at best for the beleaguered Union forces, who were pounded mercilessly by the Confederate gunners. As the day wore on,

With the shelling of Fort Sumter, the Civil War began.

the skies darkened and strong winds began to blow. Soon waves were splashing high against the walls of the old fort, bringing a new anxiety. Even though Federal ships were standing off the bar of the harbor, waiting for nightfall to bring supplies so desperately needed, how could they land in a sea like this?

Night arrived, and the winds now were almost a gale. The Carolinians had begun to use red-hot shot, a new menace. Fires broke out everywhere. Suppose one of these incendiary shells struck the powder magazine? In the wink of an eye, every man in the fort could be blown to bits!

Only the tiniest portion of fat pork remained next morning to feed the fam-

The Union surrendered the fort, now a U.S. monument.

ished, bone-weary gunners in Sumter. Still the fires raged. Still the seas rolled in great waves against dock and pilings. Still the Confederate shells rained down on the fort.

At last Major Anderson accepted the grim truth — he must surrender. Fifty guns roared out in salute to the Stars and Stripes when, the following day, Anderson and his men proudly marched out of Sumter.

Already newsboys were racing through the streets of Northern cities, shouting a single headline:

"War! War! War!"

Patriotism

What caused a riot in Baltimore?

All work stopped in those cities. People gathered to read the latest bulletins. Stunned and bewildered at first, a seething anger rose in their hearts. By the rockets' red glare, the glorious old flag of the Union had been "insulted." The Philadelphia *Press* wrote editorially: "Henceforth each man, high and low, must take his position as a patriot or a traitor — as a foe or friend of his country — as a supporter of the Stars and Stripes or of the rebel banner."

Patriotism swept like a tidal wave across the North. That Sunday practically every church steeple flew the National flag. Next day President Lincoln called for 75,000 state militiamen to serve in the National armies for three months and the response was immediate and overwhelming. Men rushed to join military companies, and quickly they embarked to guard Washington from the attack that everyone expected to come at almost any moment. The governor of Massachusetts spoke the general feeling when he addressed a company of volunteers about to board a steamer:

"You have come from the shores of the sounding sea, where lie the ashes of the Pilgrims, and you are bound on a high and noble pilgrimage for liberty, and for the Union and Constitution of your country."

The determination of the North to stand by the Union was shrugged off in the South with boasts that one Confederate could lick ten Yankees! And Southern politicians, echoing an old

chant, shouted: "Cotton is King!" How long, they asked, would foreign powers like Great Britain stand idly by if the North interfered with the South's cotton trade?

Others pursued another argument. How, really, did Southern independence change the normal way of life in the North? Once Northerners realized this fact, and thus came to their senses, how long could Lincoln sustain the wave of war hysteria now sweeping the North? All these were good questions for bolstering Southern morale, but they contained one danger. Suppose the South was wrong and the North went on fighting? Then in time the North must win, for it possessed more of everything with which to fight a war — more people, money, raw materials, factories, food, railroads, ships.

Yet Lincoln also was faced with troublesome "if's." A week after the guns at Charleston had plunged the nation into civil war, troops of the Sixth Massachusetts Volunteers reached Baltimore where they were forced to change trains for Washington. Baltimore claimed many Southern sympathizers who reacted violently to this "invasion" of Maryland's soil. In an ugly mood, they barricaded the trolley route between railroad stations.

The sight of the Union soldiers was greeted by derisive catcalls. Many cried, "Hurrah for Jeff Davis," and the cheers grew thunderous when a fellow appeared carrying a Confederate flag. Thus emboldened, the mob followed verbal taunts with a shower of brickbats. In exasperation, the Massachusetts troops fired at their tormentors and a shocked nation next morning read

A riot in Baltimore resulted when Southern sympathizers in the border city protested the presence of Union troops.

the grim score of the Baltimore riot — four soldiers dead, twelve civilians killed.

In New Orleans a school teacher who had spent happy boyhood years in Baltimore could scarcely sleep as news of the riot set his mind afire with a poem. His name was James Ryder Randall and he deserves to be remembered, for his poem, set to music, became one of the great patriotic songs rallying the South to war:

The despot's heel is on thy shore,
  Maryland!
His torch is at thy temple door,
  Maryland!
Avenge the patriotic gore
That flecked the streets of Baltimore,
And be the battle-queen of yore,
  Maryland, my Maryland!

Despite the tremendous ardor for the Southern cause that "Maryland, My Maryland" expressed, Lincoln managed to keep this border state from leaving the Union. Virginia was another story. Quickly, after Sumter, the Old Dominion State joined the Confederacy, and with her went the general the North had wanted—Robert E. Lee.

Meanwhile, both North and South, the people clamored for one great pitched battle that would end the war. Nobody then would listen to Lee, who was saying: "This war may last ten years." So, in hot July, at Manassas Junction, Virginia, the public had its way against the advice of sound military men like Generals Robert E. Lee and Winfield Scott. It learned a lesson that took years to forget.

15

Amateurs at War

North Carolina and Tennessee by now had followed Virginia into the Confederacy, and the Rebel capital had been moved from Montgomery to Richmond, Virginia. The North took up a new cry — "On to Richmond!" — but that remained a hollow threat as long as a great Confederate army under General Beauregard, the hero of Sumter, was stationed at Manassas Junction. Indeed, the advance guard of these Southern troops was at Fairfax Court House, practically within sight of the Federal capital, so that "On to Washington!" seemed even more logical.

Chock full of confidence and fight, the Union boys on July 15, 1861 marched into Virginia, determined to oust these Rebels from the doorway to Washington. Green as young apples at war, the Union lads moved off to battle as though going on a picnic. They stopped to pick blackberries. They joked and ambled along and blocked the roads over which supply wagons and artillery caissons were trying to move. To add to the confusion congressmen in fancy carriages rode out from Washington "to see the show" — everyone in the North, it appeared, believed that war was something like a baseball game.

After three days the Union troops reached a little stream called Bull Run. Here they met their first Rebels — a handful of advance pickets — who exchanged a few shots and fell back, but the great pitched battle that everyone wanted quickly developed. A red-headed colonel who later would win fame — his name was William Tecumseh Sherman — never forgot this experience "when for the first time in my life I saw cannonballs strike men and crash through the trees above and around us, and realized the always sickening confusion as one approaches a fight from the rear." And Sherman remembered also "the terrible scare of a poor Negro who was caught between our lines."

Truly, the Battle of Manassas (called the Battle of Bull Run in northern accounts) was a strange conflict. Each contending commander — Beauregard for the South and Irvin McDowell for the North — tried to swing his army around the other's right flank. Now, suppose this strategy had worked, for then, unopposed, the Northern forces would have been facing Richmond and, equally unopposed, the Southern forces would have been facing Washington!

But battles rarely go according to plan. At first the Union boys seemed to have the Rebels on the run. They rolled up a hill by the Henry House, but there met bitter opposition from Confederate General Jackson, who, an admirer said, stood "like a stone wall," and who ever after would be known in history as the immortal Stonewall Jackson. Even so, the Federal troops kept pushing hard while the Confederate lines sagged more and more dangerously, and toward mid-afternoon a great Union victory appeared in the making. But at that critical moment a second Southern army under General Joseph E. Johnston reached the field.

These reinforcements proved too

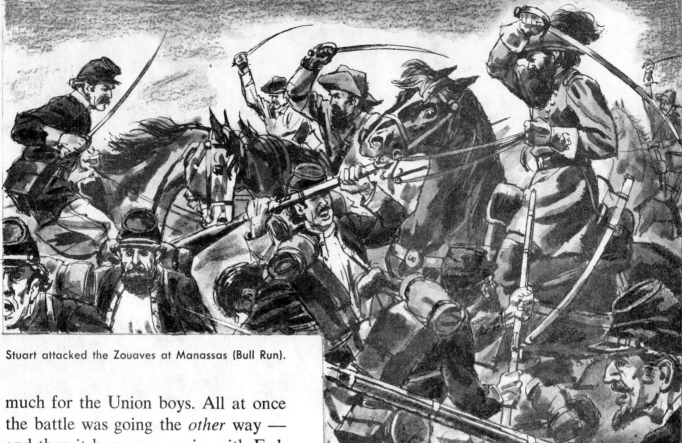

Stuart attacked the Zouaves at Manassas (Bull Run).

much for the Union boys. All at once the battle was going the *other* way — and then it became a panic, with Federal generals, soldiers and congressmen scampering like scared rabbits back to Washington. Had the Rebels pursued them vigorously, nobody knows what might have happened, but at this point the Rebs also were as green as young apples at war!

North and South, sober people read the terrible result of this battle that really had decided nothing. The Union forces at Manassas had numbered 28,-452, and now 481 were dead, 1,011 were wounded, and 1,216 were missing either as deserters or prisoners. The Confederate forces had numbered 32,-232, and now 387 were dead, 1,582 wounded, and 12 missing. But grim reading though these figures made, the bitterest part of the story was between the lines in the truth left unspoken, and which now so many people realized. This brothers' quarrel, before it ended, was likely to be long, bloody and costly.

How many battles, skirmishes and raids it took finally to end this war nobody can say for certain, but 10,000 is a fairly safe guess.

Quickly the war spread until it touched America from the Texas border to a Vermont town only fifteen miles from Canada. No hamlet along the Atlantic seacoast was safe and in the wilderness of far-off Minnesota the Sioux Indians staged a bloody uprising that Federal troops had to quell.

As the anger of the brothers deepened, and they began to fight for keeps, the war touched every ocean.

After Sumter, almost everyone had believed that the conflict could be ended in ninety days. Instead, as later events would demonstrate, America had plunged headlong into the bloodiest civil war the world ever had known!

Confederate vessels, called *blockade runners*, operated out of Southern ports like Richmond, Charleston, Savannah, Pensacola and New Orleans. Trading cotton for war supplies in foreign ports, the Rebel ships were constantly dodging Union coastal patrol boats.

What was it like to run the blockade?

On the Seas

When on April 19, 1861, Lincoln declared a blockade of the coastline of all the seceding states, some Southerners almost split their sides with laughter.

That big clown Lincoln — whom did

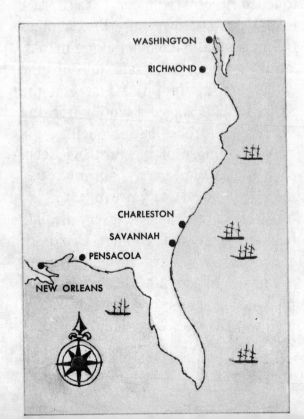

he think he was bluffing? Why, there were only three warships in Northern ports ready for action! And just suppose all ninety ships in the Union Navy were reconditioned — how did Lincoln think he was going to patrol 3,549 miles of Atlantic coast and seal off 180 Southern ports? And how about the old Mississippi — with its tributaries, Old Mis' added 3,615 miles for Lincoln's boats to patrol. Then there were sounds, bayous and rivers emptying into the Atlantic — *and* the coast of the Gulf of Mexico — in round figures, another 2,000 miles!

But Lincoln wasn't bluffing. Perhaps the President's greatest strength was the fact that he was neither the dummy nor the insincere tyrant the South was forever calling him. Rather, he was the man with a good head above his bony shoulders who possessed the heart of a lion and the tenacity of a bearcat. Take, for example, what he achieved with

the Union Navy. Maybe it had only ninety ships in 1861, but four years later it claimed 670! During the same period its number of officers jumped from 1,300 to 6,700 and its seamen from 7,500 to 51,500. In 1861 the Federal government was spending $12,000,000 a year to support its navy and by 1865 it had hiked that figure to $123,000,000!

Ultimately the South stopped laughing about Lincoln's blockade, for it was both real and dangerous. Then, alert, in trouble, the South struck back with its fleet of blockade runners. Men seeking quick, rich profits sailed these vessels under the nose of the Federal patrol in one of the most rousing series of adventures of the sea that the war produced.

For a moment, think of yourself as a blockade runner. You have taken a load of cotton to one of four ports — Nassau, Bermuda, Havana or Mata-moros — and in exchange have picked up a cargo of medicine. Now you've got to get back to a port in Georgia, and you must reckon accurately. On the average, that journey will consume three days. You consider weather and tides, for both mean life and death to you.

You're lucky — you've guessed right — and you approach the Georgian coast on a moonless night with the tide running high. You black out your ship, and cover binnacle and fireroom hatch.

"Blow off that steam underwater," you order severely, for off in that darkness — somewhere, anywhere — is the dragnet of Yankee patrol boats. Heart in throat, you drift with the tide — fingers crossed, praying hard.

Tense moments tick by. Off in the distance you hear voices — lookouts on a Federal ship changing watch. Boy, you're really praying now!

Did you make it?

Making Naval History

In February, 1862, Lincoln and his Cabinet had reason to feel as worried sick as they clearly were.

The source of their sleepless nights was the fact that when the Federal troops had left the Gosport Navy Yard at Norfolk, Virginia they hadn't done a good job. They had been ordered to destroy the *Merrimack,* one of the finest warships in the United States Navy, but the Confederates had put out the fire and now owned this magnificent ship. Moreover, as Lincoln and his Cabinet had learned to their distress, the Rebs were raising a slanting, iron-plated superstructure on the vessel's berth deck. Low and ugly, the *Merrimack* was being converted into a new kind of fighting ship designed to blow the North's wooden battle-wagons from the seas!

Against this threat, the North was gambling on what seemed like a pitiful experiment — John Ericsson's odd-shaped *Monitor* with its flat deck and squat, revolving gun turret so that it looked like "a cheese box on a raft." Some said that if the *Monitor* fought the *Merrimack,* it would be like sending a pygmy to fight with a giant.

Faces in Washington grew longer and gloomier than dark shoelaces when, on the afternoon of March 8, 1862, the *Merrimack* appeared off Hampton Roads, Virginia, flying the black flag she intended as the symbol of death to the North's wooden navy! What hours of despair followed for the Union as the ironclad *Merrimack* struck at the Federal vessels! The mighty *Cumberland* went down in flames. The *Congress* grounded in the mud and burned. The *Minnesota* also grounded, but nightfall saved her — that is, until daylight when the *Merrimack* would surely come back to finish her work of rewriting naval history.

Officials in Washington shivered in their boots, as though expecting at any moment to have the *Merrimack* come churning up the Potomac and lay waste to the National capital. But next morning the *Merrimack* was again off Hampton Roads. Then, suddenly, "a little black mass" appeared — the *Monitor.* On came Ericsson's queer vessel.

It was difficult for those who watched that famous sea battle to believe what they saw. Broadside after broadside fired by the *Merrimack* seemed only to bounce off the *Monitor* until in despair one Southerner admitted the truth: "It's like so many pebble-stones thrown by a child!" Meanwhile the *Monitor* was far from idle. Her turret spun around and dropped open a port cover. Out popped an eleven-inch gun. Boom! The gun sprang back. The port cover slammed shut. There was nothing to hit!

Through the morning the pygmy duelled the giant, and at last, badly sagging, the *Merrimack* limped back to Norfolk. The North cheered the *Monitor,* and soon men were smoking cigars named "El Monitor"! Great Britain suddenly looked with respect at the Federal Navy, for she hadn't a first-class ship that could stand against Ericsson's spunky little freak.

The greatest naval battle of the war took place between the South's *Merrimack* and the Union's *Monitor*.

Professionals at War

Like a dog cooling its nose, a strip of Virginia between the York and James rivers rests in the waters of Chesapeake Bay. Called the Peninsula, this strip of land in 1862 provided a natural highway to Richmond and the heart of the Confederacy.

Traveling up the Peninsula was like journeying through the pages of American history. At Yorktown stood the battleground where George Washington had won a decisive victory over the British redcoats under Lord Cornwallis. In Williamsburg were streets that once had echoed with the footsteps of Thomas Jefferson and Patrick Henry.

In all America there was not more sacred ground, and, along roads that Washington once had ridden, a Federal army of 110,000 under General George B. McClellan drove toward Richmond in the spring of 1862.

General McClellan's Army of the Potomac was the greatest fighting organization ever assembled on the American continent. Whenever it moved, the effect was the same as though a city like Albany or Indianapolis, with all its people, horses, wagons, food and ambulances, had moved. It even carried balloons with which to send soldiers into the sky to spy on the enemy.

McClellan was no amateur at war. Trained at West Point, he already had won a victory for the North in the mountains of western Virginia and his soldiers believed in him. But he was slow and cautious and confused, believing reports that the Confederates opposing him were at least twice as strong as they actually were. He distrusted Lincoln, with whom he bickered constantly. Still, mile by mile, McClellan ground his way up the Peninsula until the sound of his guns was distinctly heard in Richmond.

Robert E. Lee, who served an inconspicuous role in the war as a military advisor to Jefferson Davis, watched in agony this slow advance of the Union troops. Confederate forces on the Peninsula were under the command of Joseph E. Johnston, who had saved Beauregard in the battle at Manassas Junction, but now Johnston kept falling back on Richmond without offering a firm stand against McClellan. Where,

who would live forever as the heroic symbol of the South. In character, Lee went to work almost around the clock. He suspected that the right wing of McClellan's army was "in the air" — that is, unsupported — and he called Stonewall Jackson with his army in the Shenandoah Valley to come to the defense of Richmond.

On June 28, 1862 Lee launched his attack against McClellan, bringing on a series of related actions that became known as the Battle of the Seven Days. Through tardiness on Jackson's part in putting his troops into action the first day, the Confederates suffered terribly at Mechanicsville. Lee kept his head, marched Jackson's forces through the night to where he wanted them, and next day battered the Union army at Gaines' Mill.

Lee believed that he had licked McClellan and could easily crush or capture his entire army, but McClellan was shrewder than Lee suspected. This Union general loved every man in his army as though he were a son, and to save his army McClellan rose to heights of defensive greatness. Now he did what Lee had not considered possible — he moved his army across the Peninsula to where it could be under the protection of Federal gunboats on the James River.

So, as so often occurs in war, success and failure had followed in rapid succession. Lee had saved Richmond but McClellan had slipped through his fingers. The end was not in sight.

when, Lee asked anxiously, was Johnston's retreat to stop? At a meeting of the Confederate Cabinet, Lee spoke with tears running down his cheeks:

"Richmond must not be given up — it shall not be given up!"

Yet McClellan was in trouble. Heavy rains endangered the Union's bridges across the Chickahominy River, and finally on May 31, 1862 Johnston was persuaded to strike an exposed flank of McClellan's army. The vicious Battle of Seven Pines that resulted seemed to decide little, but its impact upon the war was enormous since Johnston was wounded and the supreme command of the Confederate forces passed to Lee.

The South had found its man of history and of legend — the immortal Lee,

Fight for the Rivers

How did a boat win a land battle?

Meanwhile there was a great deal of war elsewhere in America. Pioneers had moved along rivers to build a country, and now soldiers fought over those same rivers to control the country.

Increasingly a new name was in the headlines — the name of a squint-eyed, stump of a general known as Ulysses S. Grant. Schooled at West Point, where he had stood last in his class, Grant appeared out of nowhere to win decisive victories, first capturing Fort Henry on the Tennessee River and then winning Fort Donelson on the Cumberland.

Union mortar rafts in the
river fired on Island No. 10.

April of 1862 brought more disheartening news to the Confederacy from the Tennessee River. At Shiloh, in a surprise attack, the Confederates had seemed on the point of crushing Grant, but like Lee, he also had kept his head and turned disaster into victory.

Other disheartening news awaited the South that April. In Missouri, 17,000 Union troops under General John Pope cast covetous eyes upon Island No. 10, below Columbus, Kentucky. This island, which the Confederates had fortified, was the key to controlling the upper Mississippi River, and Pope wanted it badly.

An old wooden gunboat called the *Carondelet* — "she looks," said her skipper, "like a farmer's wagon" — was,

however, the Union's actual hero in the battle for Island No. 10. The moon was lost behind an approaching thunderstorm when, on the night of April 10, the old *Carondelet* swept down the river with chain cable wrapped around her pilothouse for armor. On Island No. 10 bugles summoned the Rebs to battle-stations in the fort.

On came the *Carondelet* through the rains that now pounded down. The guns of the creaking gunboat flashed in the darkness. But the Rebs only saw her briefly — when her own guns barked death or when lightning streaked the sky. Overhead the thunder rolled.

It was a fearful scene, really — the guns of the *Carondelet* pounding the fort, lightning, the thunder. And when it was over, Island No. 10, with 7,000 Confederate prisoners of war, was surrendered to General Pope.

How did some
old cigars change
Lee's plans?

Maryland, My Maryland

Since men rather than boats receive official credit for winning land battles, General Pope, as the hero of Island No. 10, was brought east to command the Union forces defending Washington. A man of strange moods and too many words, Pope bragged of the victory he would win. He issued orders that were senselessly harsh upon civilian Virginians, and whereas he may not have won many friends, he at least succeeded in making one bitter, unremitting enemy.

That foe was Robert E. Lee, who loved Virginia and Virginians more than life itself. Lee was certain that McClellan, though still on the Peninsula, had no intention of again attacking Richmond. Boldly, Lee decided to move southward and handle once and for all the high-handed, loud-talking Pope.

In a series of brilliant moves, Lee so confused Pope that the poor fellow at one point was actually marching and counter-marching his army in an aimless circle. Finally, on August 30, 1862, Lee caught Pope in battle at Manassas Junction (called the Battle of Second Manassas or Second Bull Run) and so thoroughly thrashed his hated adversary that Pope soon was heading back west to live in relative obscurity for the remainder of the war.

Again Washington quaked for its safety, expecting momentarily to see the Rebel army storming at its gates. But Lee had a bolder plan. He would carry the war entirely away from the soil of his beloved Virginia.

After all, there was strong pro-Southern sympathy in Maryland — or so Lee believed, at any rate — so why wouldn't many Marylanders welcome his army as liberators? He would divide his army, sending one wing under the ever reliable Stonewall Jackson to capture Federal troops and supplies at Harper's Ferry, Virginia. Meanwhile Lee hoped to strike across Maryland into Pennsylvania, where by seizing the railroad bridge over the Susquehanna River at Harrisburg he could cut off communications between the North and the West except by the slow, roundabout route over the Great Lakes.

With his bands playing "Maryland, My Maryland," Lee marched his army across the Potomac. Then Lee, who was filled with surprises for the North, began to experience a few surprises himself. First, the Marylanders who watched his moving columns were far more hostile than friendly. Next, a

The Blues crossed Burnside Bridge at Battle of Antietam.

strange accident occurred and a copy of Lee's secret order, revealing his full plan, was found wrapped around some cigars by a Union sergeant. McClelland, back in command, danced with joy at learning Lee was separated from Jackson. He'd get Lee this time, McClellan boasted jubilantly.

Unexpectedly McClellan struck Lee in a savage battle at South Mountain that ended at nightfall. For all the advantage McClellan had in surprising Lee, the best he could claim for that engagement was a draw.

Lee pulled his army back to Sharpsburg, crossing the stone bridge over the Antietam River and forming in line of battle between the town and the stream. McClellan, ever the hesitant, delayed a day and threw away his advantage, for now Jackson, flushed with a smashing victory at Harpers Ferry, came storming over the hills to reinforce Lee.

Next day, September 17, 1862, the armies clashed in "the bloodiest day of the war." In the damp, chilly dawn the Battle of Antietam began along a sunken road that the soldiers renamed the "Bloody Lane." Around a little white Dunkard Church, across the stone bridge, through a cornfield, the battle swept in blazing fury.

The air, said a Union army surgeon, was "vocal with the whistle of bullets and scream of shells." The cornfield, said a Confederate general, "looked as if it had been struck down by a storm of bloody hail." McClellan had reserves that he never employed that might have turned the day into a disaster for Lee, and nobody knows for sure why they were not used. Nightfall mercifully closed the carnage of this fearful day when each side counted its casualties at about 10,000.

On the following day, like a general stunned into numbness, McClellan made no move to renew the contest. A day later Lee started for home, murmuring as his troops recrossed the Potomac: "Thank God!" He knew how lucky he had been.

The Year of Jubilo!

What were Lincoln's thoughts as he watched the spiders?

Since after Antietam the Southern forces had retreated into Virginia, Lincoln decided to regard the engagement as a "victory." The President was seeking an excuse to take a bold action that changed the entire purpose of the war.

Lincoln had been considering this course since June, when on many days he would arrive at the telegraph office in the War Department and sit quietly at a desk. Before him was a pile of paper on which, occasionally, he would write a few words, but for longer periods of time he would simply gaze out the window, lost in thought. A colony of spiders that lived in webs on the outer window fascinated the President and he came to know all their habits. Often he stopped to read the latest war dispatches — not always the most cheering news. At the end of each visit he carefully locked the desk so that no one could read what he was writing.

The pile of paper grew in the desk, and then one day in mid-July, riding in a carriage with the Secretaries of Navy and State, Lincoln revealed his mystery. Should the South persist in carrying on the war, the President said, he had decided to free the slaves as a matter of military necessity. Later at a Cabinet meeting the Secretary of State warned Lincoln not to issue his proclamation without a military success to support it or else the people would look upon his proclamation as "the last measure of an exhausted government." Lincoln couldn't deny that the secretary's argument made sense, so once more the papers were locked in a desk.

Now the Battle of Antietam — with Lee on the run — gave Lincoln the opportunity he wanted and five days later he issued his first, or preliminary, Emancipation Proclamation in which he warned that if the regions then in rebellion did not return to the Union by January 1, 1863, he would issue a second proclamation declaring slaves in those regions to be "forever free."

The South reacted violently. Some angry Southerners went so far as to cry that the time had come at last for the Confederacy to raise the black flag of piracy and offer the North no quarter! In the North, however, many were overjoyed by Lincoln's Proclamation.

With sound logic Southerners argued that the Emancipation Proclamation, by itself, couldn't free a single slave. Again, as in the early days of the blockade, the South taunted the President. Whom did he think he was bluffing? But once again Lincoln wasn't bluffing. He was reaching out — touch the hearts of people around the world — lifting the war above a legal argument to a ground where it became a crusade for human freedom. His proclamation, wrote workingmen in England who had suffered from the loss of Southern cotton, was a "triumph of

Lincoln's "Emancipation Proclamation" declared free all slaves in states still in rebellion against the Union.

justice, humanity, and freedom," and they would stand by him no matter what sacrifices they had to make!

Single-handedly, really, Lincoln had won the first true victory of the war. He was saying in legal language what Northerners sang in their churches in "The Battle Hymn of the Republic":

*As He died to make men holy, let us
    die to make men free,
While God is marching on!*

29

Lee, the Invincible

What great disaster struck the South after Chancellorsville?

Not by any means had Antietam knocked the fight out of Robert E. Lee. Rather, it was the Federal commander who seemed to be inventing endless excuses for not pursuing Lee, and Lincoln decided at last that he had suffered enough of McClellan's "slows." So the Union's powerful, big Army of the Potomac was placed under the command of another general — Ambrose E. Burnside, who wore copious side-whiskers and rode smartly on a bob-tailed horse, but who frankly admitted that he did not believe he was qualified to command an army.

And Burnside was right. Over hills that George Washington had roamed as a boy, Lee's army and Burnside's collided in mid-December, 1862 in the Battle of Fredericksburg. The core of that battle was a hill that the Yankees had to approach across a sunken road.

Atop Marye's Heights, protected by a stone wall, were Confederate guns ready to belch death at any assault.

Six times Burnside ordered his loyal troops up Marye's Heights. Six times the Union boys charged and six times the Rebel guns rained down a storm of lead upon them.

It was a ghastly sight, truly — the dead of one charge piling upon the dead of the charge that had gone before. Wave upon wave, the brave Bluecoats tried to storm Marye's Heights, and each time the Confederate guns were like scythes cutting down rows of wheat.

Once a single Yankee came within a hundred yards of the wall that shielded the Rebel artillery. There, for a moment, his comrades saw him — an heroic, defiant figure, waving his arm. Then he, too, was dead — just another sacrifice on that dreadful day.

Federal troops met defeat at Chancellorsville by Confederate forces under Robert E. Lee and Stonewall Jackson.

Jackson was accidentally shot by one of his own men.

Lee said at Fredericksburg: "It is well that war is so terrible — or we should grow too fond of it!" Staggered, the North read the reports from Fredericksburg. The Union's casualties had numbered 12,653, those of the Confederacy, 5,309!

When the third spring of the war arrived, the Army of the Potomac had a new commander in General Joseph E. Hooker. In Lincoln's eyes he possessed one virtue that outweighed any shortcoming — he was willing to fight. In April, with the Virginia dogwood in bloom, "Fighting Joe," as he was called by his troops, moved suddenly above Fredericksburg, boasting that Lee and his soldiers had better pack their haversacks and make for Richmond.

Lee let Hooker march into Chancellorsville on the edge of that desolate region of Virginia known as the Wilderness. In this tangle of stunted oaks, where only owls, whippoorwills and water moccasins could long survive, Lee met Stonewall Jackson on May 1, 1863. Together, they planned an unpleasant surprise for Hooker. While Lee held the front with only a relatively small force, Jackson would march the remainder of the army by a little known road around Hooker's right wing and crush the unsuspecting Federal troops before they could realize what had happened.

The plan, as brilliant as any the war produced, worked perfectly. Jackson crashed down on Northern troops with their arms stacked, preparing supper, and in the dusky twilight shattered them. Raw, nasty fighting still remained at Chancellorsville, but the Union forces never recovered their balance after Jackson struck.

Yet even as another great victory loomed, Lee lived through the days that followed in agony, for Jackson had been shot by accident by his own men. Stonewall's arm was amputated, and for a time he seemed to recover, but then pneumonia developed.

"God will not take him from us, now that we need him so much," Lee prayed.

But "Old Jack" had fought his last battle. His death plunged the South into tearful mourning.

Hooker's losses at Chancellorsville were 16,845 against 13,156 for Lee. Receiving this news, Lincoln paced the floor of the White House, moaning: "My God! My God! What will the country say?"

Was there no general in the North who could win against Robert E. Lee?

Indeed, there was — just one.

Grant and Vicksburg

"He's hopelessly stuck in the mud," critics said that spring of General Ulysses S. Grant.

Grant did seem bogged down since he had brought his army from Memphis and camped on the high ground above the city of Vicksburg. This city, set on high bluffs above the Mississippi, was ringed with formidable batteries, for the Confederates knew that if they lost Vicksburg, they would lose control of the most important river in America.

To add to Grant's troubles, high water in the tributaries of the Mississippi that spring had covered wagon roads to a depth of seventeen feet. But Grant tipped back on a camp stool, puffing on a cigar and thinking hard. The only way to win a war, Grant decided, was to do the unexpected.

And that was precisely what Grant did. If fortifications made Vicksburg impregnable to a frontal assault, then he would have to come at it by the "back door." So, loading his army on transports, he took it down river under the blazing guns on the bluffs of Vicksburg.

Grant knew that the Rebel army under General John C. Pemberton within Vicksburg waited to be reinforced by another army under Joseph E. Johnston — a juncture that he must prevent. Grant knew also that the rules of war declared an army must operate from an established base of supplies, but Grant decided to write his own rule-book. He would live off the land as he fought, cutting his way between the armies of Generals Pemberton and Johnston.

Quite before the Confederates had guessed what was happening, Grant had captured Mississippi's state capital of Jackson, wedged his army between Pemberton and Johnston, beaten back Pemberton's army in a fierce battle at Champion's Hill, and followed Pemberton to the "back door" of Vicksburg.

Here, however, he was stopped cold in two terrific assaults in late May. Again Grant tipped back on his camp stool, thinking. If you couldn't win with bullets, then you had to win with bellies. He would besiege Vicksburg and starve out its defenders.

For six weeks, shells from Grant's cannon and gunboats pounded Vicksburg — as many as 150,000 on a single day, some said. Homes, churches, schools, stores, factories were smashed into rubble. Soldiers, old men, women and children dug caves in the hillsides as Vicksburg was renamed the "Prairie Dog's Village."

A baby, born twelve feet underground during the siege, lived to tell the tale. Every day became like Sunday to those living in the caves. Food became so scarce that people even sipped a broth made of tree buds simmered in water. When the shelling stopped, folk piled up heaps of iron fragments, just for something to do.

Yet, stubbornly believing that Johnston and his army were coming to their help, the people hung on. Surrender? Never! In time they even grew accustomed to the shelling, and when Grant's guns renewed their fury, they grinned as soldiers ordered:

"Rats, to your holes!"

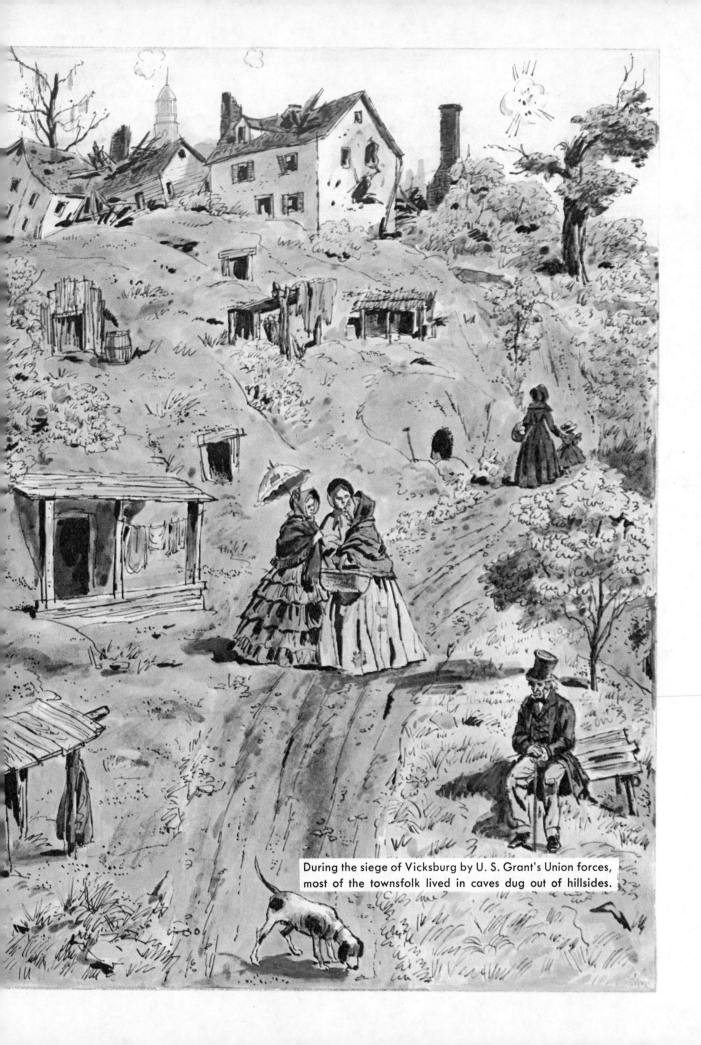

During the siege of Vicksburg by U. S. Grant's Union forces, most of the townsfolk lived in caves dug out of hillsides.

Why did a general
ask Lee not to fight
at Gettysburg?

Gettysburg

In Richmond, Jefferson Davis faced the truth. Unless relief could be sent to Pemberton, sooner or later Vicksburg must fall. General Lee was summoned to an emergency meeting of the Confederate Cabinet. Should troops from the Army of Northern Virginia be sent to Vicksburg? Lee, always first a Virginian, shook his head. He spoke feelingly of what two years of war had meant to his proud old state — farms stripped of food, houses falling apart. His army needed everything — shoes, food, horses. Where could he find them? Lee mentioned the magic word: "Pennsylvania!"

So Lee again invaded the North. "It's like a hole full of blubber to a Green-

lander," cried one of Lee's generals on beholding the rich farm lands of the Keystone State. Unhappily for Lee, his cavalry under Jeb Stuart became so entranced in chasing toward Washington to capture a Federal supply train that contact was lost with the main army. Lee had lost his "eyes" — the job of the cavalry, in such situations, is to spy out and report the position of the enemy — and Lee could not know that hard on his heels came the Army of the Potomac under still another commander. He was General George Gordon Meade, Pennsylvania-born and resolutely determined to defend the soil of his native state.

Unexpectedly, on July 1, 1863, the two armies collided near the sleepy village of Gettysburg. Lee's boys fought magnificently, rolled over Union troops caught in a railroad cut, and sent them flying on their heels through the town. A vigorous pursuit might easily have turned the day into a rout, but the Rebs stopped instead to celebrate their vic-

Lee's Confederates in Pickett's Division stormed Union entrenchments at Gettysburg, but were driven back.

tory. Union troops that night occupied a height known as Cemetery Ridge.

Next morning, seeing the Yankees dug in on those slopes, General James Longstreet advised Lee to get out of Gettysburg. This was Fredericksburg in reverse, Longstreet insisted, with the Union holding the upper hand. But flushed with yesterday's success, Lee wanted to stay and fight. Scorching battles fought in sultry heat under overcast skies that day wrote strange names into American history — Little Round Top, Big Round Top, Devil's Den, the Peach Orchard, the Wheatfield — and here Billy Yank died beside Johnny Reb when night closed upon a contest still undecided.

Lee did not lose heart. On July 3 his cannon opened a terrific bombardment that stunned the Yankees on Cemetery Ridge. Then across 1,400 yards of open ground he sent the boys in Pickett's Division to storm the Union forces in their entrenchments.

Row on row the Rebs came, steady, brave, willing to risk anything Lee asked — then the Yankee guns spit flames of fire, and the rows of grayclad soldiers seemed to melt away. Others came up to take their places. Again the guns flashed, again the Rebs dropped, until all at once the utter hopelessness of Pickett's Charge swept over them and they turned and ran for dear life.

A courageous man waited as the Rebs reeled back across the field. "Don't be discouraged," General Lee called gently. "It was my fault this time." A faint smile touched his lips and he said: "All good men must hold together now." That night Lee began his weary retreat to Virginia. Three days at Gettysburg had cost him 3,903 dead, 18,735 wounded, 5,425 missing. The Union's loss was 3,155 dead, 14,529 wounded, 5,365 missing.

A staggering blow for the South was Gettysburg. And next day — July 4, 1863 — brought an even more shattering blow when Vicksburg and Pemberton's army surrendered to Grant.

Mid-Country

Why did the North idolize Grant?

In September before Chattanooga, Tennessee, a Confederate army under Braxton Bragg beat back a Federal army under William Rosecrans in the Battle of Chickamauga. To this trouble spot rushed Grant. Finding the Union soldiers facing starvation or surrender, he forced open a supply route — his famous "cracker line." Then in November at Missionary Ridge in the "Battle above the Clouds" Grant's angry, snarling boys charged up steep hillsides, drove through ravines and overran Rebel riflepits until the Confederates, in Bragg's own words, were seized by "a panic which I never before witnessed."

Who now could deny one fact? In Grant the North at long last possessed a *winning* general.

In the Battle of Lookout Mountain near Chattanooga,
Union soldiers captured the fortified stronghold.

Grant vs. Lee

Why did soldiers love them both?

Congress revived the rank of lieutenant general, previously bestowed only upon George Washington and Winfield Scott, and in March, 1864 Lieutenant General Ulysses S. Grant was called to Washington to take command of all Union armies in the field. In round figures, Grant commanded 533,000 soldiers — a fighting force then without an equal in American history — and Grant's first move was to confer with his old friend, General William Tecumseh Sherman. They would divide the country, Grant said. While Sherman took the western armies and smashed his way to Atlanta, Grant would "handle" Lee in the East.

In early May, Grant threw the great Army of the Potomac, which totalled 125,000 men at full strength, against Lee's Army of Northern Virginia, which did not number more than 60,000. The first battles were fought in the desolate Wilderness, where Hooker had met disaster. In this wolf's den death came unseen among the oak thickets, for this was a contest fought more by ear than by eye. "It was not war," a witness said. "Two wild animals were hunting each other. When they heard each other's steps they sprung and grappled."

But Grant was no Hooker, no Burnside, no McClellan. He knew how to use reserves — "feeding a fight," he called it — and Lincoln believed in him implicitly. Asked what was happening to Grant, the President replied cheerfully: "Well, I can't tell you much about it. You see, Grant has gone into the Wilderness, crawled in, drawn up the ladder, and pulled in the hole after him, and I guess we'll have to wait till he comes out before we know just what he's up to."

What, actually, was happening in the Wilderness proved a bitter lesson to Grant. Lee could fight — great guns, how Lee could fight! — and Grant was losing men two to one. But where other commanders of the Army of the Potomac always had pulled back when Lee had walloped them, Grant simply sought more favorable ground on which to continue the fight. Thus Grant began his famous "sidling to the left," a maneuver that pulled Lee after him until they were out of the Wilderness. Old soldiers in the Army of the Potomac cried happily, "Boys, we're on our way to Richmond!"

Lee's soldiers were devoted to him. "Well, boys," said a Rebel one day, "the rest of us may have developed from monkeys, but I tell you none less than God could have made such a man as Marse Robert!" And how those hungry, war-weary, outnumbered Rebs fought for Lee — piling up the Union dead in heaps at Spotsylvania, following doggedly after Grant across the North Anna, the South Anna, the Pamunkey, then catching him at Cold Harbor and inflicting such dreadful losses that a shocked North began talking of "Grant, the Butcher!"

"I was wrong," Grant said after Cold Harbor. He was a big enough man, this Grant, to admit a mistake. If his "smash-'em-up" tactics wouldn't work against Lee, then he'd have to try something else. One thing was sure, he wouldn't retreat, for since boyhood, taking any step backward had made Grant feel dizzy!

So Grant began on June 15 to race Lee around Richmond to Petersburg. Here both armies dug in within sight of each other for a stubborn siege that dragged through hot summer into a brisk fall, and then through a bleak and chilly winter into the spring of 1865.

Lee grew into a legend, and in Richmond there was talk about making him military dictator of the Confederacy. He was now the "Noble Lee," the old gray warrior who had been knighted in heaven and who, sharing the discomforts of army life, kept his sense of humor. Once when he was calling on Mrs. Davis, and she brought him coffee in a fine China cup, he said good-naturedly: "My cups in camp are thicker, but this is thinner than the coffee."

Grant bogged down before Lee — the Confederacy took heart. But from the West came disastrous news. By a series of brilliant flanking maneuvers, Sherman had driven the Confederates out of Atlanta! Then from 3,000 miles away, and from Mobile Bay closer by, came word of Union naval victories that lifted Northern spirits and disconcerted McClellan, who that fall opposed Lincoln for re-election as President. The Democrats had placed their entire strategy on branding "Mr. Lincoln's War" a failure. But Sherman and Admiral John A. Winslow and Admiral David Farragut suddenly had cut the legs off that claim!

Grant's Union Army suffered tremendous losses in his Wilderness campaign fought at New Cold Harbor, Va.

The War Takes a Turn

Atlanta smoldered in ruins, burned by Sherman and his soldiers. "Where is Sherman?" a puzzled North began to ask, and even Grant admitted with a grin that his red-headed friend had disappeared like a mole under a lawn.

> **Why did Sherman disappear?**

Sherman knew where he was going — clear across Georgia to the sea. Taking a lesson from Grant at Vicksburg, he would make the country feed him as he marched. The South had started this conflict, growled Sherman, and now it could feel "the hard hand of war." And Sherman said a great deal more that the South remembered bitterly — for

Atlanta was burned by Sherman soon after city fell.

example, how he would make "all Georgia howl."

You had to know Sherman's nervous temperament, and probe beneath his extravagant words, to realize that he was one of the shrewdest, best generals in America. As a boy he had so hated his red hair that he had tried to dye it, but his hair had turned green, so he had learned to live with it. Sherman was like that — hard-headed and practical, knowing that wars ended only when the resources for waging war were destroyed. And that was what he proposed to do — to go deep into the South, and destroy its capacity for making war.

In six weeks — tearing up railroads, burning any building that resembled a

Gen. Sherman marched through Georgia to the sea.

military installation (and a great many that did not), raiding plantations to feed his carefree, hungry "bummers" — Sherman cut a path of destruction across Georgia. Wheeler's cavalry and the local militia could offer only token resistance. Negroes shouted, "We's gwine whar you'se gwine, massa," and by the hundreds they followed Sherman's victorious columns. At night the Negroes staged plantation dances and sang spirituals until after a time Sherman's boys insisted that the march to the sea was "just about as much fun as a fox hunt."

Comparing Sherman to a ground mole, Grant had added: "You can here and there trace his track, but you are not quite certain where he will come out till you see his head." Suddenly Sherman's head appeared, and he had reached the sea at Savannah. At once he sent Lincoln a telegram:

"I beg to present you as a Christmas gift, the city of Savannah, with one hundred and fifty heavy guns and plenty of ammunition, and also about twenty-five thousand bales of cotton."

"Many, many thanks for your Christmas gift," Lincoln replied, adding a confession: "When you were about to leave Atlanta for the Atlantic coast, I was anxious if not fearful; but feeling you were the better judge, and remembering that 'nothing risked nothing gained,' I did not interfere."

41

For Lincoln the war was going swimmingly. But a big problem remained — how to end it.

How did the Federal Navy help re-elect Abe Lincoln?

The Confederacy's answer to the Union's naval blockade was to set loose upon the seas armed raiders to prey upon Northern merchant ships. The most successful of these was the *Alabama,* under command of Raphael Semmes, which during her career sent about sixty vessels to a watery grave and cost Yankee shipping a loss of approximately $6,500,000.

To find and to sink the *Alabama* became the dream of the United States Navy, and so shouts of joy arose from the Yankee crew of the *Kearsarge* when they sailed into Cherbourg on June 14, 1864 and found the *Alabama* at anchor in the French harbor. The *Kearsarge* waited off the breakwater for the *Alabama* to come out, and news of the impending battle brought eager spectators by excursion train from Paris.

They were not disappointed in the "show." On a bright, warm Sunday — June 19 — the lookout on the *Kearsarge* shouted: "She's coming out, and heading straight for us!"

When the two ships were 900 yards apart, Winslow, aboard the *Kearsarge,* ordered his first broadside. In a series of seven overlapping circles, the *Alabama* and the *Kearsarge* duelled. Winslow's boys, by far the better gunners, took their time — aiming deliberately, pounding home the shot from their 11-inch guns upon the *Alabama's* hull, piling the dead on her decks. Semmes knew his days as a raider had ended. Up went the white flag.

Then on August 5, 1864 a Federal fleet under Admiral David Farragut

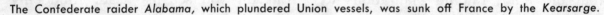

The Confederate raider *Alabama*, which plundered Union vessels, was sunk off France by the *Kearsarge*.

sailed into Mobile Bay. This old sea horse, who had been a midshipman in the United States Navy at the incredible age of nine, already had won fame by capturing New Orleans in 1862. As still an open port of the Confederacy, Mobile Bay was equally a prize and Farragut meant to have it.

At 5:45 next morning, when the fog lifted on a promising day, Farragut ordered his fleet into action. Disaster struck quickly when a torpedo plunged the lead ship to the bottom of the bay. Reputedly Farragut shouted: "Damn the torpedoes — go ahead!" And putting his flagship in the lead, Farragut pounded his way past the blazing guns protecting the bay.

Now came the real fight as the Rebel iron ram *Tennessee* came out to smash Farragut's wooden ships. Straight for the Federal flagship, the *Hartford,* she headed. Union monitors swarmed around the *Tennessee* like snarling sea-dogs, and Farragut had himself lashed to the rigging to command the battle.

Eight-inch plates protected the *Tennessee*. Iron covers closed over her gun ports. But soon the *Tennessee* learned why Farragut was renowned. A Union shell knocked off the *Tennessee's* stack. Another jammed the cover over her port gun. A third smashed the leg of her admiral. Suddenly the *Tennessee* ran up the white flag. Farragut had knocked out the pride of the Rebel navy and Mobile Bay was won!

For Gideon Welles, Lincoln's Secretary of the Navy, it had been a fine summer indeed, and he felt at long last that he had avenged the poet who early in the war had written:

Admiral Farragut won a naval victory at Mobile Bay.

Retire, O Gideon, to an onion farm,
Ply any trade that's innocent and slow,
Do anything, where you can do no harm.
Go anywhere you fancy — only go.

Now Welles could say that he had done more than his share — for the country and for Lincoln, standing for re-election. The impact of such triumphs as sinking the *Alabama* and capturing Mobile Bay — along with Sherman's occupation of Atlanta — surely would be felt when the voters went to the polls in November.

Many advisors had pleaded with Lincoln to cancel the election, in view of the national emergency, but he had shaken his head. The people must decide. They ran the government. Now on election night the President sat in the telegraph office of the War Department awaiting that decision. Early returns from Boston, Philadelphia and Baltimore were encouraging. And then toward midnight, as more and more of the vote was counted, Lincoln knew — he would carry every state except Kentucky, Delaware and New Jersey and win by an electoral vote of 212 to 21!

With Malice Toward None

Where was
the final
victory won?

Actually wars are not won on battle-fields, but in the hearts and minds of men — sometimes in the heart and mind of one man, if he happens to be Abraham Lincoln.

One such victory Lincoln already had won when, through the Emancipation Proclamation, he had given a moral purpose to the war, and now on January 31, 1865 he won an even greater victory. Ten months earlier the United States House of Representatives, voting on a Thirteenth Amendment that would prohibit slavery throughout the nation, had failed to give the two-thirds vote necessary for passage. Lincoln, however, had interpreted his re-election as a mandate from the people to get on with the real work of the war, and had thrown his full influence behind bringing the Thirteenth Amendment to another vote.

The signs all looked favorable. In recent weeks slavery had been abolished in Arkansas, Louisiana, Maryland and Missouri, and similar legislation was pending in Tennessee and Kentucky. So spectators crowded the galleries of the House when, at 4:00 o'clock, that last day of January, Speaker Colfax ordered another roll call on the Thirteenth Amendment. Anxiously, senators left their own chambers and crowded around the door to the House. Name by name, the congressmen voted. The tally clerk whispered the result to Colfax — Ayes 119, Nays 56. The amendment had passed by sixty-three votes!

Congressmen, leaping to their feet, danced in the aisles. The galleries burst into thunderous cheers and outside a battery boomed a hundred-gun salute. Lincoln could not disguise his pleasure. Passage of the Amendment, in its way, he said, "winds the whole thing up." He congratulated everybody — himself, Congress, the country, the whole world.

"The Battle Hymn of the Republic" had not been meaningless after all: "As He died to make men holy, let us die to make men free." For the dead at

"With malice toward none; with charity for all . . ." Thus spoke Lincoln at his second inaugural address when he was re-elected.

Gettysburg and Vicksburg and ten thousand other places, there was a purpose.

Afterward, awaiting his second inaugural, Lincoln seemed to draw within his own thoughts, as though searching, searching, searching for the words to say one thing more that was in his heart and mind. On the morning of March 4, 1865 drizzle filled the gusts of wind from an overcast sky. Then Lincoln arose to speak — just as the sun burst through. And standing there in the golden light, he described the great triumph that the country had yet to win:

"With malice toward none; with charity for all; with firmness in the right, as God gives us to see the right, let us strive on to finish the work we are in; to bind up the nation's wounds; to care for him who shall have borne the battle, and for his widow, and his orphan — to do all which may achieve and cherish a just and lasting peace among ourselves, and with all nations."

The crowd watched as the tall man took the oath of office, then stooped and kissed the Bible. Old Abe — the man to whom they sang:

We are coming, Father Abraham,
Three hundred thousand strong . . .

And come they had — and would still — and neither they, nor their children, nor their children's children would ever, ever forget how he had touched their lives and changed their common destiny.

To Appomattox

Only once during the entire war did the three men who shaped its final victory — Lincoln, Grant and Sherman — meet face to face. The place was the steamer *River Queen,* anchored off City Point, Virginia. The date was March 27, 1865, and Sherman's "bummers" were marching northward through the Carolinas on their way to join Grant's forces at Petersburg. Lincoln hoped that the war could be ended without another costly battle, but neither Sherman nor Grant could give the President much hope on that score. Grant, leaving for Petersburg next morning, told an aide:

"I think we can send him some good news in a day or two."

Within a week Grant had smashed through at Petersburg, the Confederate government had fled southward, and Union troops had occupied Richmond. Lincoln visited the Confederate capital on April 4. "Thank God I have lived to see it," he said. Negroes by the hundreds ran to meet him, and Lincoln told them: "Learn the laws and obey them." Almost like a small boy, he sat in the chair which Jefferson Davis had used for so long in running the war against him. And to the Federal commander in Richmond he gave characteristic advice: "Let the people down easy."

Lee still believed that he had a chance of escaping from Grant on that April day when Lincoln visited Richmond. He drove hard for Amelia Court House, where he expected to find supplies for his hungry soldiers. They were not

there. For five days, on courage alone, Lee carried on the struggle, but Grant's well-fed, buoyant troops were all around, pressing Lee into the little pocket of mountain countryside around Appomattox Court House and blocking the way on flank, front and rear. Officers pleaded with Lee: "Fight on!" Sadly Lee faced the truth:

"There is nothing left me to do but to go and see General Grant."

On Palm Sunday — April 9, 1865 — Lee rode into Appomattox to meet Grant not as a foe, but once more as a countryman. The two great generals of the war shook hands. Quietly, as gentlemen, they discussed terms of surrender that would be fair, under the circumstances. The documents were written out and Lee read them carefully, once borrowing a pencil to make a small insertion.

"I felt like anything rather than rejoicing at the downfall of a foe who had fought so long and valiantly," Grant said afterward.

At last the papers were ready to sign. Again, the generals shook hands. Lee went out on the porch of the McLean House, where the meeting had occurred, and called for his horse. As Lee mounted, to ride off, Grant came onto the porch and raised his hat. Lee returned the salute.

Lee's army saw him coming back. The soldiers of the Lost Cause now rushed to the roadside, crowded around him, shook his hand.

"Uncle Robert!" some shouted.

"God help you, General," others cried.

Lee's throat tightened. He had to

Lee surrendered to Grant at Appomattox, Virginia.

wait some moments before he could speak only these few words:

"Men, we have fought through this war together. I have done the best I could for you. My heart is too full to say more."

He turned then and strode to his tent — to be alone with his thoughts, his grief for the stricken South.

So the war was over. Some men shouted and danced. Some wept. Some wondered anxiously about the nation's future. One who faced that future bravely and wisely was Lincoln. On Good Friday, April 14, he spoke to his Cabinet:

"We can't undertake to run State governments in all these Southern States. Their people must do that — though I reckon at first some of them may do it badly."

With malice toward none, with charity toward all . . . Lincoln knew how the future of the country must unfold. But that night a dreadfully unbalanced man assassinated Mr. Lincoln, and at 7:22 the following morning the President died. Looking down on Lincoln's face, at peace in death, a voice at the bedside spoke softly:

"Now he belongs to the ages."

And the South had reason to grieve with the North, for it too had lost a friend — a great friend.

What did the war achieve?

Brothers Again

The war had cost a staggering price. The Union counted its dead at 360,222, its wounded at 275,175. The South had 258,000 dead by a fair estimate. No one could guess how many Southerners had been wounded.

For what purpose? That, really, we knew deep in our hearts. In November, 1863, Lincoln had gone to Gettysburg to dedicate a National Cemetery. What the war must achieve he stated clearly:

". . . that this nation, under God, shall have a new birth of freedom — and that government of the people, by the people, and for the people, shall not perish from the earth."

Many of the problems that had plagued the country before the war still remained, but one did not. Slavery was gone and at long last the Negro in America had begun to be an American.

And we found something more — under all the anger, in the midst of all the fighting. We found ourselves. We came together, and the boy in blue who died beside the boy in gray in battle were really the same boy. In other wars, when the nation was threatened, they would stand side by side.

Poets know how to say these things best — and one who said it well was Frank Lebby Stanton:

After all,
One country, brethren! We must rise or fall
With the Supreme Republic. We must be
The makers of her immortality —
Her freedom, fame,
Her glory or her shame:
Liegemen to God and fathers of the free!

Stanton was born in South Carolina, the first state to secede from the Union.

"One country, brethren" — North and South — was the brotherly spirit voiced by many after the Civil War.